CUT OUT ALONG THE DOTTED LINE & AROUND EACH ENVELOPE LINER

CUT OUT ALONG THE DOTTED LINE & AROUND EACH ENVELOPE LINER

CUT OUT ALONG THE DOTTED LINE & AROUND EACH ENVELOPE LINER

CUT OUT ALONG THE DOTTED LINE & AROUND EACH ENVELOPE LINER

CUT OUT ALONG THE DOTTED LINE & AROUND EACH ENVELOPE LINER

CUT OUT ALONG THE DOTTED LINE & AROUND EACH ENVELOPE LINER

CUT OUT ALONG THE DOTTED LINE & AROUND EACH ENVELOPE LINER

CUT OUT ALONG THE DOTTED LINE & AROUND EACH ENVELOPE LINER

CUT OUT ALONG THE DOTTED LINE & AROUND EACH ENVELOPE LINER

CUT OUT ALONG THE DOTTED LINE & AROUND EACH ENVELOPE LINER

CUT OUT ALONG THE DOTTED LINE & AROUND EACH ENVELOPE LINER

CUT OUT ALONG THE DOTTED LINE & AROUND EACH ENVELOPE LINER

CUT OUT ALONG THE DOTTED LINE & AROUND EACH ENVELOPE LINER

CUT OUT ALONG THE DOTTED LINE & AROUND EACH ENVELOPE LINER

www.ingramcontent.com/pod-product-compliance
Lightning Source LLC
Chambersburg PA
CBHW081159070526
44583CB00021B/2912